The Pocket Guide to

SETTING UP AN INTERIOR DESIGN BUSINESS

David Wisson

The Pocket Guide to
SETTING UP AN INTERIOR DESIGN BUSINESS

The Pocket Guide to
SETTING UP AN INTERIOR DESIGN BUSINESS

Copyright ©

By David Wisson

The Pocket Guide to
SETTING UP AN INTERIOR DESIGN BUSINESS

The Pocket Guide to
SETTING UP AN INTERIOR DESIGN BUSINESS

Table of Contents

Copyright ©..3

Introduction 6

What is interior design 11

      Materials and Coverings..14

The different styles of interior design 16

Bohemian style of interior design 17

Scandinavian 18

Farmhouse 19

Industrial...20

Victorian..21

The Basic Building Blocks of an Interior Design Business 22

Identify and Understand Your Market. 22

Develop your Interior Design Business...............................23

Make your Interior Design Business Available and Desirable to your

Market. 25

The advantages of marketing your Interior Design Business: 27

Other things to think of to help your business...................29

A Web Site 29

Summary 32

And Finally...33

The Pocket Guide to
SETTING UP AN INTERIOR DESIGN BUSINESS

The Pocket Guide to
SETTING UP AN INTERIOR DESIGN BUSINESS

Introduction

This pocket guide will give you an overview on how to Setup an interior design business. If you are successful and put in the time, effort and research, then there is no reason why you should not be able to achieve a significant income from your interior design business.

This pocket guide has been designed so that it is easy to read and to understand, without any of the technical verbiage associated with writing and language so a novice interior designer can get started with little or no experience in the field of interior design.

I will give you a brief outline of what an interior design business entails is the different type's interior design depending on the style that you chose. Of course, the client's views are paramount but your business should be built around your style and personality. This is what will get you noticed and bring you your biggest rewards. Interior design is one of the most flexible, diversified fields and can be a very lucrative business to engage in.

Operating your interior design business can be managed to suit your lifestyle needs such that it can be operated on a full time, part time, even a temporary basis. Interior design is a varied business because you can consider many different facets of interior design in your business or you can limit yourself to only one aspect or niche of it. Interior design can be very lucrative because fees for such consultation and services can be high, and there are many opportunities to make additional revenue from the fabrics and furnishings used as part of the job.

As a starting point, you should consider specializing in one particular area or style such as early Tudor decoration and antiques, or Victorian decor and furniture or something more radical like Scandinavian interiors and furniture or even the Urban Modern look and feel. However, there is no reason why you to should start out with such bold specialist, particularly in the early stages of your business. You can grow slowly and securely into the niche that you have chosen.

You do not need expensive office space or studios; you can easily and happily control and conduct the business from your home. Learning the basics of your craft is always a bonus, as it will give you confidence and the knowledge to blossom in your business rather than floundering around not knowing the path to follow. You should try and attended adult education classes in interior design or take some sort of formal qualification training, as this business will be more than a casual interest, especially if you are bidding for high earning projects. It is of particular note that the kitchen and bathroom are the two rooms that most people tend to neglect; however, they are the rooms that any potential buyer will remember the most. You can earn a good living from that small snippet of information. You should learn and understand all about the following, as they are essentials in your trade.

- Colour
- lighting
- blueprint reading
- proportion
- mood
- room traffic and flow
- furniture
- arrangement
- period furnishings
- woods
- fabrics
- patterns and textures
- and much, much more.

It will be very helpful for you to have an understanding of curtain making and the styles that curtains can be made in. In addition, a small amount of upholstery work will enable you to estimate materials and measurements accurately.

If you have all of these attributes, you will feel more qualified to decorate almost any room to both your satisfaction and your customer's joy.

The ultimate goal of the interior decoration is to provide an appealing combination of colours, a comfortable arrangement of harmonious furnishings with the details and accessories, which reflect your skilful but personal and professional touch. As is too often the case, one well-done job leads to many recommendations as talk of your ability spread.

What is interior design

People are spending more time indoors, be it due to climate change, unwelcome conditions outside or the latest pandemic to hit the world. All of these affect our lives, our well-being, and especially our health. Designing an interior of a house or property is an honour that few professionals get to achieve as an interior designer and is a great responsibility.

As an interior designer you need to do your homework for your customer and this entails research, planning, organising, and managing the project so that you capture your customer's vision in an aesthetically pleasing and healthy environment for your customer and the individuals that will frequent the environment on a daily basis.

Interior design is the amalgamation of the customer's colours, coverings, and finishes. This is only part of the overall picture that you are trying to capture from your customer.

It is imperative to understanding the use of the space and the customers' requirements to create a well-designed and visually pleasing environment. The flow of people through the space and the gathering places within it is and ideal place to start. This can be done by capturing your customer's views and requirements in a small but effective survey. Interior designers must also pay close attention to the environmental conditions within the space being redesigned. This covers such things as heating, lighting and soundproofing where required. Layout of fixture and fittings as well as the positioning of furniture in a room is an important part of the overall design.

A good Interior design layout, will consider all of the building regulations and standards that have to be applied to the project and demonstrate compliance to disabled accessibility standards and emergency egress where required, such as fire escapes and safe areas.

Materials and Coverings

It is important to select your finishing materials carefully as all materials should comply with the relevant safety regulations. Your choices should not only be ruled by factors such as price, purpose or function and looks. The choice of the finish to be selected is complex and individual to the customer and must meet your customers' requirements and needs. The following aspects in the design should be considered:

The space usage

Consider the amount of traffic that will flow through the area. The layout must consider the most practical layout for its function. Is the area easy to clean and keep tidy? There is nothing worse than an untidy and dirty space, which is hard to clean due to the furniture arrangement. To fully appreciate and understand interior, factors such as lighting, colour and textures can affect the look and feel of a space and make it welcoming. If you get it wrong, you may make the space uninviting or even cold and lifeless.

Interior design is not about knowing how to make a room, flat or apartment or house look pretty. It is about understanding your customer and their needs and desires. Not everyone will use a space in the same way, depending on his or her height or his or her size and each person feels comfort in a different way. It is important to have an overarching approach and managing your project like a true project manager when designing your interiors. You should consider the happiness, and the health of your customer, be it the person paying you for your service or the person inhabiting the space that you have designed. This is how to achieve a successful Interior design project.

The different styles of interior design

There are a vast number of interior design styles. They are only limited by your imagination. You can if you want to, start your own niche in interior design by blending two different styles of interior design and renaming it to your own style or brand. I have collated a number of different styles below to give an overview of just a couple of the styles out there.

Bohemian style of interior design

The Bohemian style of interior design tries to encapsulate the happy-go-lucky and daring principle of the modern lifestyle. It practices the artistic use of vibrant colours and bold designs, featuring colour-matching sets such as red or purple or green and yellow pallets. The look the designer is trying to represent is the organised untidiness look. The designer is trying to achieve the warm atmosphere look and this is achieved by layering textiles such as fabric-covered furniture, covered with occasional throws and skater cushions and pillows. The Bohemian style of interior design uses expensive looking rugs covering polished wooden floor, with classy art and tapestry hanging on the wall.

Scandinavian

The Scandinavian interior design style gave the world a minimalist design look that is forever timeless. The Scandinavian interior design style features contoured furniture, subdued colour pallets, and a variety of complimentary organic and engineered Materials and Coverings. The style of Scandinavian furniture can be described as simple or even basic but is modern, and practical. Scandinavian interiors can be decorated sympathetically in shades of white with grey overtones as the complimentary colour.

Farmhouse

Farmhouse decor is a contemporary style, which reflects the country living with a minimalist approach using wood and warm textured materials and coverings. The furniture style in a Farmhouse interior design is inspired by the distressed wood look and upholstered in dark linen or felts. Natural whites and beiges are used as a base colour on the walls and ceilings and complimented by brightly coloured throws and pillows or cushions.

Industrial

The Industrial interior design style gives a style that looks back to the industrial era at the turn of the twentieth century. In terms of the overall feel, the industrial decor style is often rustic and mature. The use of bare untreated steel complimented by old wooden furniture, wooden flooring and exposed brickwork with copper-tone accents makes the look and feel of this style a must have for the young modern executive.

Victorian

The Victorians pioneered many of the iconic designs that influence today's modern society. They produced many of the splendid buildings that still stand as testament to their design around the world. They demonstrated the use of refined lines, simple shapes that epitomised the Victorian interior design style. Interiors were plush and extravagant with brightly coloured frills and accessorise, complimenting grand furniture and warm open fires.

The Basic Building Blocks of an Interior Design Business

Identify and Understand Your Market.

Begin with market research by looking investigating discretely, the other Interior Design Business and look at what others are doing. Look at the different types of Interior Design business niches are currently available to you.

Look out for the Interior Design Business niches that no one in your region or area seems to be interested in. Make your service better by standing out from the rest. Offer something new, which will get you recognised.

Develop your Interior Design Business.

Recognise the potential of an untapped market and make it your Niche. Begin to specialise in the area that you have identified. Your Interior Design Business subjects could range from Victorian to Edwardian or Modern to Minimalist, the choice is yours.

You can always find an underdeveloped niche in most Modern service provision markets today. However, it is always best to go with the style that you know most about and can talk about it and 'sell' your Interior Design Business to a discerning customer.

You may not last very long if you chose a field that you have little or no knowledge or experience in and you cannot stir the juices of passion for.

Even though you could specialise in one area, it should not limit you to one particular Interior Design business style.

You should be able to discover plenty of opportunities to work in other areas or niches and subjects to help build your business.

Make your Interior Design Business Available and Desirable to your Market.

Develop a marketing strategy to target potential clients in the niche field you have developed.

Reach your targeted market audience by displaying your Interior Design Business online and by leafleting potential customers. Promote your website in every way that you can and provide flyers and business cards with the web address on it. Use SEO to improve your ranking on Google and link to other design websites and ask for reciprocal links.

Display Interior Design Business posters at the events and venues such as the good home exhibition around the country, which you really must attend. Provide quality examples or samples of your Interior Design work that your business has undertaken. It is always best to try to get requests for work and orders for your Interior Design Business at these venues, which will keep the money flowing in. In addition, you should take your own reference photographs from your Interior Designs portfolio that you or your company have undertaken. Within no time, your order books will be full and you will have amassed an extensive collection of related photos and materials for your website.

Interior Design Business can be a gift for those working in the target Niche. They can be an especially attractive business for the husbands or wives and family of people working within the Niche, who are willing and able to assist and earn a wage form the business. These resources can be utilised as your business grows.

The advantages of marketing your Interior Design Business:

Marketing your Interior Design Business enables you to promote your business to a particular group or niche target audience that is actively looking for your Interior Design niche.

It allows you to concentrate your efforts on enhancing your knowledge and customer base. As your knowledge in the industry grows, your business will become more uniquely recognisable, and improve your Interior Design reputation.

By focussing your marketing efforts you can effectively reach the specific audience for your Interior Design, you can increase your sales while gaining recognition as an expert within that field. That recognition brings more opportunities for the sale of your business to your customers. As time goes on and you become an expert in your field, you could generate different income streams by doing things like online workshops via your website and even produce publications, and more on particular Interior Design styles in which you specialise.

You do not necessarily need premises when you first start out, your business could be operated entirely from your home. The creation of a good website and the use of a decent digital camera can give your customers an idea of the Interior Design range on offer by your company on your website.

Other things to think of to help your business

A Web Site

As we have mentioned previously, a website is a place where you can showcase your craft and allow prospective customers to view the work that you have previously undertaken. This is also an ideal platform to display your reviews that you get for your work.

With today's online e-solutions, you can quickly and easily create a website on the internet with all of the bells and whistles flashy images and other things to make it attractive to potential customers. Use PayPal or a similar e-Money system to allow your customers to pay for the service and extras that you offer such as curtains, cushions, desirable objects and ornaments and any additional work that you undertake.

Do not let a website daunt you. A modern web hosting

company such as '1and1' or 'Hostgator' (there are many other providers out there) provide you with all of the tools to enable you to build your own professional looking website in just a couple of hours. There are many different templates that you can use, which will help you to achieve just the look and brand that you want.

Having a website, with links to other platforms that you are advertising through such as Facebook, Twitter and other social media platforms on the internet, can drive new customers to your website to give them the inspiration to start their own projects with you as the lead.

Remember to make your website interesting and functional. Provide interesting facts about the subjects and styles that your business is covering and make it inspirational to hold the visitors interest and provide a link so that they can contact you for information and potential work.

The Pocket Guide to
SETTING UP AN INTERIOR DESIGN BUSINESS

Provide your reader with interesting information about yourself and how you got started in the interior design business. Have clear and correct navigation links to all of the pages on your website and to the other websites that you are connected to. Have an easy to use and simple shopping cart system, which enables effortless checkout without having to think about it for the additional products that you may want to sell such as soft furnishings and bespoke lighting etc... In this way, customers who have a positive experience will come back again and hopefully purchase a second or third product from your site and even commission you to undertake their Interior Design project.

The Pocket Guide to
SETTING UP AN INTERIOR DESIGN BUSINESS

Summary

An interior design business offers an entirely new business opportunity for the enterprising budding interior decorator. Yes, this type of business is well known and there is a great deal of compensation at the mainstream end of the market but it is the niche that you have identified that provides the opportunities to start and develop your interior design business. Those of you with good skills, knowledge and experience with a niche area that needs exploiting, can develop a successful interior design business.

And Finally

This pocket guide has been written to whet your appetite and to give you that push that you have been looking for to start your 'Interior Design Business'. This guide is not an exhaustive guide and cannot guarantee you success in your venture. There is no doubt that there are many more areas required to setting up a successful business that this guide does not cover. Never the less, if you put the time and energy into making your interior design business your passion, I am confident that you will make a success of your venture.

Printed in Great Britain
by Amazon

35923631R00020